ArtScroll® Youth Series

Rabbi Nosson Scherman / Rabbi Gedaliah Zlotowitz
General Editors
Rabbi Meir Zlotowitz ז״ל, *Founder*

POLICE
Published by
ARTSCROLL
Mesorah Publications, ltd

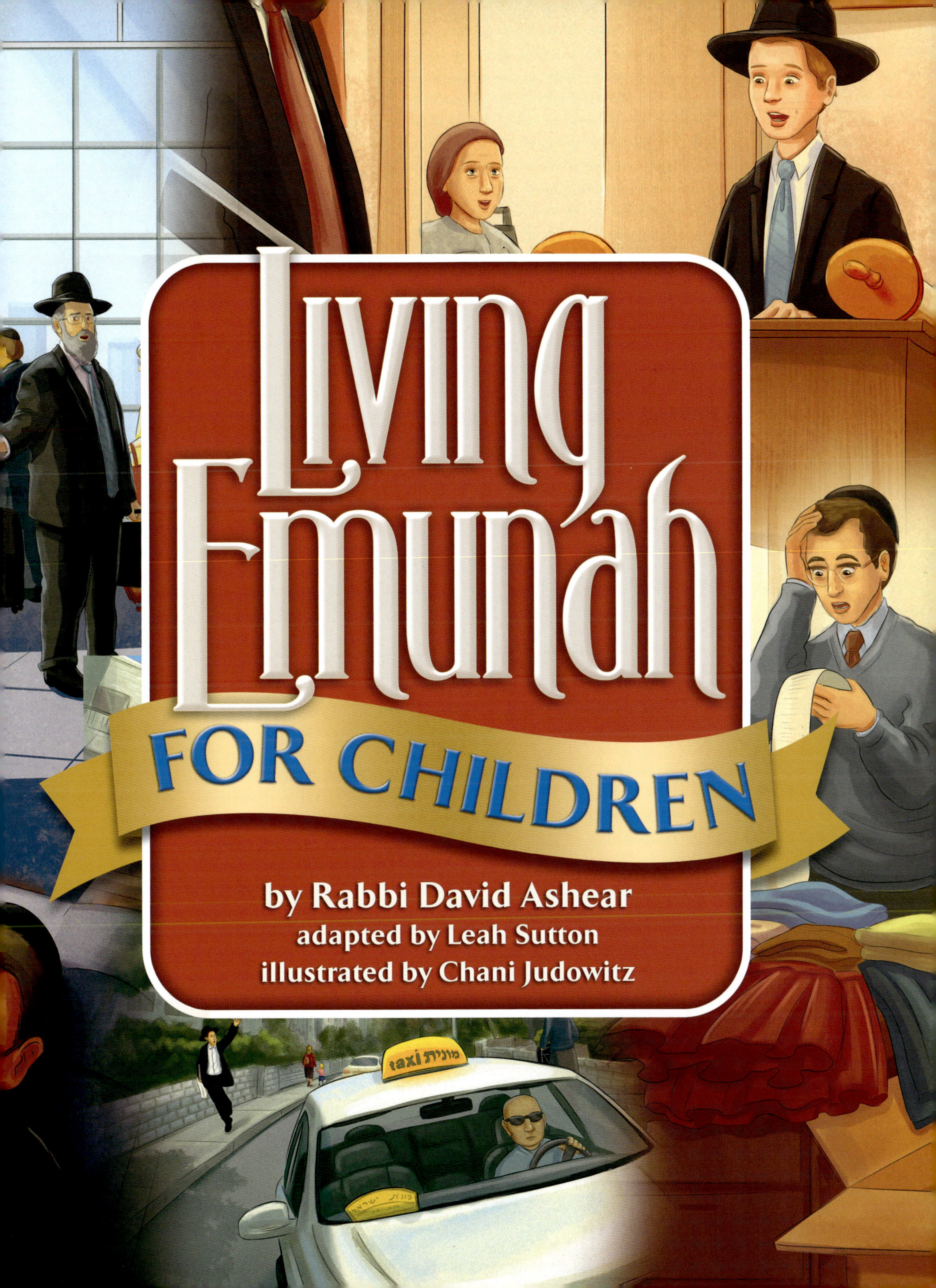
Living Emunah
FOR CHILDREN
by Rabbi David Ashear
adapted by Leah Sutton
illustrated by Chani Judowitz
taxi מונית

L'iluy nishmas

Refoel Yisroel ben Yehuda Tzvi

RTSCROLL® YOUTH SERIES

"LIVING EMUNAH FOR CHILDREN"

First edition – Five impressions: November 2017 — June 2022
Sixth impression: November 2023

Published by **MESORAH PUBLICATIONS, LTD.**
313 Regina Avenue / Rahway, NJ 07065 / (718) 921-9000 / Fax: (718) 680-1875
www.artscroll.com

Illustrated by Chani Judowitz.

Distributed in Israel by **SIFRIATI / A. GITLER**
POB 2351 / Bnei Brak 51122 / Israel / 03-579-8187

Distributed in Europe by **LEHMANNS**
Unit E, Viking Business Park, Rolling Mill Road / Jarrow, Tyne and Wear / England NE32 3DP

Distributed in Australia and New Zealand by **GOLDS WORLD OF JUDAICA**
3-13 William Street / Balaclava, Melbourne 3183 / Victoria, Australia

Distributed in South Africa by **KOLLEL BOOKSHOP**
Northfield Centre / 17 Northfield Avenue / Glenhazel 2192 / Johannesburg, South Africa

Printed in PRC

ISBN-10: 1-4226-1946-X / ISBN-13: 978-1-4226-1946-9

Dedicated by **Jack and Sonia Gindi**

for the success of our daughter

Marilyn Rae Gindi

Dedicated in loving memory of

Stella Liniado ע"ה

Our beautiful Stella,

Your full-of-life spirit and angelic beauty will live forever in all of us.
You are a shining example of what a daughter is.
We love and miss you forever.

ת.נ.צ.ב.ה

Love,
Mommy, Daddy,
Marc, Justin and Michael

Dedicated with heartfelt gratitude to Hashem for blessing us with such wonderful children.
May He bless them with health and happiness.
And may He give them *siyata dishmaya* to reach their potential in His *Avodat Hakodesh*.

I would like to thank **Hashem** for guiding this project throughout.

A special thanks to the people who worked hard to bring it to reality: **Rabbi David Sutton** for coordinating this project; **Leah Sutton** for choosing and adapting the stories from *Living Emunah*; **Rabbi Nosson Scherman** and **Shmuel Blitz** for their editorial input; **Chani Judowitz** for her delightful illustrations that make the stories come alive; **Devorah Cohen** for her beautiful page layout and cover design; **Mendy Herzberg** and the entire **ArtScroll team**; lastly, the generous sponsors. May this book be accepted by the public and inspire children to a life of Emunah.

Rabbi David Ashear

Table of Contents

Introduction
Emunah — Beyond the Right Words

Do we and our children believe in Hashem?
What a foolish question! Of course we do!
Are we satisfied with our level of emunah?
Well — there's always room for improvement.
How often do we see Hashem in our everyday lives?
Every day? No, not every day.

But we say three times a day in *Modim* that Hashem performs *miracles* for us *every single day.* The challenge for all of us is to recognize His presence in our lives, and to raise our children to have such faith as they grow up. Our grandparents and great-grandparents lived with *emunah peshutah,* pure and simple faith. How can we achieve that for ourselves and especially for our children?

Rabbi Yechezkel Levenstein, the great *mashgiach* of the Mirrer and Ponevezh yeshivos, gave his young daughter a notebook and asked her to write down every time she saw Hashem's *Hashgachah Peratis* (Divine Providence) in her life. She thought it would take her a long time to find even a few such things. But as time went by, she realized that Hashem was helping her more than once every single day — and the notebook began filling up. For the rest of her life, she saw the hand of Hashem day in and day out.

In this book, you will find stories that will teach our children how to see Hashem's hand in our lives all the time — if we just open our eyes to look for Him. The stories are gripping, the writing is beautiful, the message is valuable. Our children will love the book, and as parents we should seize the opportunity to let them absorb messages that will enhance their lives as long as they live.

Rabbi Nosson Scherman

Time Will Tell

The whistle blew as the train arrived at the London station.

Yosef was on his way to his weekly 9 o'clock choir practice. He entered the train and took a seat. He had rushed out of his house making sure he would not be late.

The train left and Yosef took out a *sefer* to learn.

"I am so hungry," he thought. He looked at his watch and saw that it was only 8:30. "Great. I have plenty of time. I will get off at the next stop and buy myself a cup of coffee. I will still get to choir practice on time."

At the next stop Yosef walked off the train and walked toward the coffee shop. Then, suddenly…

BOOM!!

There was a giant explosion. A terrorist had blown up the train!

Yosef was in shock. He could not believe what had just happened.

People were running in every direction. Sirens wailed in the distance as police cars made their way to this most recent terror attack.

Yosef took out his phone and tried calling his parents. But he was not able to get a connection to tell them he was okay. He knew how worried they would be. Surely they knew he was on that train.

He walked for two hours, finally arriving home.

"Yosef, you are okay," his mother shouted, tears streaming down her face, hugging him tightly.

His father closed his eyes, and thanked Hashem. "We are so grateful. We knew you were supposed to be on that train at 8:50 when it exploded."

POLICE

Yosef looked at his parents, perplexed. "No. The explosion was not at 8:50. It was at 8:30. I know because I had just looked at my watch to make sure I had enough time to get off the train to buy a cup of coffee and still be at choir practice on time. If I had not gotten off the train I would not be alive now."

Now his father looked confused. "But we heard on the news that the explosion happened at 8:50."

Yosef looked at his watch. He could not believe his eyes. The watch still said 8:30. He realized that if he had known it had been 8:50, he would not have left the train. He understood that Hashem had saved him, by making his watch stop working.

Later that day, he visited his Rav, Rabbi Farhi, and told him this miraculous story. He was overjoyed.

"Take a picture of this watch now," Rabbi Farhi told Yosef. "If you ever want to be sure that Hashem runs this world, just look at the picture of your watch. Then you will remember."

Hashem has many ways to take care of us. Sometimes, we do not realize it right away, but He is with us every second of every day.

A Fearless Flight

Six-year-old Chani walked down the aisle of the airplane, rolling her little pink carry-on behind her. She arrived at her seat and asked the woman sitting next to her, "Would you please put this on top for me?"

"Of course," she answered, a big smile crossing her face.

The woman was happy to help. She felt that Hashem was making sure that there was someone there to keep an eye on the young girl.

All the passengers found their places, buckled their seat belts, and the plane took off into the sky. Chani came well prepared. She was ready with her coloring book, crayons, and favorite doll.

Suddenly, the plane began to shake. "Attention all passengers," the pilot announced over the loudspeaker. "We are flying through some very bad weather. Please make sure your seat belts remain buckled and do not get up from your seats."

Many people on the plane became nervous. But Chani just kept smiling and remained calm. She continued playing with her doll.

The plane veered left and right. It bounced up and down, fighting the strong winds. Passengers became more and more nervous. Some began to cry. Others began to pray. The woman next to Chani held tightly onto her seat. The knuckles on her hand were white from squeezing her armrest.

But Chani was not frightened at all. She looked around at the people on the plane and thought, "Why are all these people so afraid? There is really no reason." And she continued playing with her doll.

Finally, the plane passed the stormy weather and flew peacefully on to Israel.

As the plane rolled to a stop on the ground, the woman turned to Chani and asked, "You are alone on this plane. You have no one here with you. How did you stay so calm during all that terrible weather?"

She smiled and answered, "My father is the pilot. He is the best pilot in the whole world and he is taking me home. Why should I be afraid?"

Children feel safe in the hands of their father. All of us are like young children in the hands of our Father in Heaven — Hashem. When we believe that, we will always feel safe, no matter what is happening around us.

Payback

Efraim looked at his watch as he waited for a taxi. He didn't realize how late it was because he had been caught up in the *gemara* he was learning. He needed to get home quickly.

A taxi driver stopped and Efraim hopped into the back seat. "10 Shimshon Street," Efraim told the driver. He pulled out his *sefer* and continued learning.

The taxi arrived at his house. "Thank you," Efraim said to the driver. He got out and walked toward his front door, still thinking about the *gemara*. The taxi zipped away.

Suddenly, Efraim stopped in his tracks.

"Oh, no. I forgot to pay the driver," he realized.

Meanwhile, the driver also realized that Efraim had not paid him. "He seemed so nice," he thought. "I guess he has a lot on his mind." The taxi driver decided to just look for his next customer.

Efraim ran after the taxi as quickly as he could. He chased it from one corner to the next. Every time the taxi stopped at a red light Efraim thought he would catch it. But the light turned green and the taxi continued driving.

Finally, Efraim caught up. Totally out of breath, he knocked on the window and the driver rolled it down.

"I forgot to pay you!" Efraim panted. "I'm so sorry! Here's the money."

The driver was shocked. "What?!? You chased me all the way until here?" He could not believe that Efraim had run so far just to pay him.

taxi מונית

Thirty years passed by. Efraim noticed a sign in his shul saying that a famous rav would be giving a speech about *Kiddush Hashem*. It sounded interesting and he decided to come and listen.

The rav spoke beautifully. He explained that when someone makes a *Kiddush Hashem*, Hashem lets that person see all the great things that happened because of it.

When he had finished, Efraim approached the rav and asked him, "Thirty years ago I made a *Kiddush Hashem* and I haven't seen anything happen because of it." He told the rav about how he had chased the taxi driver in order to pay him.

The rav heard the story and shouted, "I cannot believe this. I am that driver!"

He told Efraim, "As soon as I saw how honest a *yeshivah bachur* was, I decided to become religious myself. I started learning and I became a rabbi all because of you! Right now, Hashem is showing you the wonders that came from your mitzvah!"

There are times when nobody sees us do a mitzvah. But we know that Hashem sees everything and rewards us for each mitzvah that we do.

Print Shop Problems

Reb Simchah Gross was a happy man. He owned a successful print shop in Bnei Brak. But what he loved most was going to the *shiur* of the Chazon Ish each morning.

One day, on the way to his shop, he saw workers putting up a sign for a new store. He smiled. He hoped the new owner would be very successful.

Reb Simchah returned to his own shop and began working.

It was the end of the day. "Good night, Reb Simchah," his worker called from the door.

Reb Simchah smiled back at him. "Have a good night."

Suddenly, the worker rushed back in!

"Reb Simchah!!" he cried. "Another person is opening up a print shop down the street. He will take away customers. Let's bring him to a *beis din*. He is not allowed to do this!"

Reb Simchah stopped him. "Don't worry," he said softly. "Hashem is in charge of how much money we earn. It is all in His hands."

But that night, R' Simchah could not sleep. He worried about earning enough money to feed his family. Then he remembered what he had told his worker. "Hashem is in charge of how much we earn."

He decided not to fight with this new competitor. R' Simchah fell asleep and dreamed peacefully.

The next morning after the *shiur*, he entered the new print shop down the street.

He looked around. The new store looked much nicer than his. He walked over to the new owner and shook his hand warmly.

“May you have much success,” he said. “My shop is a few doors down. If you ever need anything, come right over. I’ll be happy to help you.”

The new shop owner was surprised. Another person might have been angry. But not Reb Simchah. He knew that no one can take away what Hashem plans to give someone.

> *We should all try to be like Reb Simchah. Sometimes we might think that someone wronged us. But we should not get upset. We should trust that no one can do anything bad to us if it is not what Hashem wants.*

Happiness Will Help

Mordechai Koplovitz was very poor. He lived in a broken shack with his wife and children. The cold winds blew in through the cracks in the kitchen window

Mordechai worked as a plumber. Each day he waited for work. Some days he would fix a sink, on others a broken pipe. Some weeks he got many calls to fix things. Other weeks, almost no one called. During those weeks, his children were hungry and cried. His wife would worry.

This week, nobody called. There was no money. It was already Thursday night and there was not even one potato in the house!

"What will we eat for Shabbos, Mordechai?" His wife asked.

Mordechai was so sad. He did not know what to do or say. He turned to Hashem.

"How will I feed my hungry family?" Mordechai begged. "I did everything that I could. But if You decide that we shouldn't have food for Shabbos, I will happily accept what You want."

His worries fell away. Mordechai was happy with whatever Hashem chose for him. He went to bed and fell asleep quickly and peacefully.

He had been sleeping for just a few minutes when there was a loud knock at the door! "Who could be knocking so late?" Mordechai wondered. He washed his hands and opened the door. The town's richest man stood there.

"Are you Mordechai the plumber?" he asked.

"Yes, I am," he replied, wondering why the man would visit him so late at night.

"Well, Mr. Koplovitz, we need your help right away. I own the bathhouse. A main water pipe burst. We must get it fixed before people come to shower for Shabbos!"

Mordechai couldn't believe his ears. This was just what he needed!

He worked through the night. The sun rose just as he finished. The pipe was fixed. The people in the town would have a place to bathe for Shabbos.

The rich man paid him well. Mordechai ran to the market to buy challah, wine, and chicken for Shabbos. And the family had a wonderful Shabbos.

We must fully trust Hashem and accept that whatever He does is good and best for us. And that is when He will help us even more!

Moshe's Medicine

Little Moshe lay in bed coughing. He was very sick. He was burning up with fever. His mother pressed a cool wet towel on his forehead.

In the morning she called the doctor to come and see him.

The doctor examined Moshe and looked worried. He quickly wrote a prescription and told the mother, "You must get this medicine right away. Your son's life is in danger!"

She gathered all the coins she could find and ran to the closest pharmacy. She begged Hashem to make the pharmacist accept the small amount of money that she had. There was no more.

"Please," she cried. "Have pity on my son! I don't have enough money to pay for the medicine. Take these coins. It is all I have."

The owner was not there, but his assistant smiled and said, "I can do that for you." He prepared Moshe's medicine and handed it to her.

She ran back home holding the bag tightly to her chest. Suddenly, she stepped into a small hole in the sidewalk – and fell! The bottle with the medicine broke and it all spilled onto the ground.

"Oh, no. What will be now?" she moaned! "I don't have money to pay for more medicine!" Sadly, she picked up the bag with the pieces of broken glass and returned to the pharmacy.

This time, the owner was there. Sobbing, she told him the story and that she had no money for more medicine.

The kindhearted man said, "Do not worry. I will give you more medicine for free!" He took the bag with the broken bottle. He smelled it, and then his face turned white.

DRUGS
PHARMACY
est. 1890

“I cannot believe this,” he cried. “Hashem was protecting you today! My assistant gave you the wrong medicine. It would have made your son even sicker.”

She was overjoyed. She understood that Hashem was protecting her son.

Little Moshe grew up to become the great Rabbi Moshe Sherer, leader of Agudas Yisrael, who helped thousands of Jews all over the world.

Even when everything seems terrible, we must believe that Hashem has a plan and is doing it all for our good.

Torah Can't Harm You

The Machaneh Yehudah market in Jerusalem is always crowded with people. Rabbi Yaakov Yagen owned one of the many small shops there.

Every night he would wake up at 2 o'clock in the morning and learn with the great *mekubal (*a Rabbi who studies the secrets of the Torah), Rav Mordechai Sharabi. When the sun rose, they would *daven Shacharis* and continue learning Torah for a few more hours.

Reb Yaakov opened his shop at 11 o'clock each morning. The other shops in the market opened much earlier, at 6 o'clock, but he was busy then learning with Rav Sharabi.

"Don't you think it would be better if you opened your shop earlier?" his wife asked. "If you open your shop when the others do, you would make much more money."

Reb Yaakov asked Rav Sharabi what to do. The Rav smiled. "The same Hashem Who sends you money at 6 o'clock can also send it to you at 11 o'clock. If you are learning Torah, Hashem will take care of you."

Reb Yaakov was happy. He continued to go to his shop every morning at 11 o'clock.

One man noticed that every morning people were outside Reb Yaakov's shop, waiting for him to open. He had an idea.

"I will open a store right next to Rabbi Yaakov Yagen and sell the same items that he sells. But I will open up at 6 o'clock. His customers will come to me instead," he thought.

He got to work quickly. He opened his store at 6 o'clock with a big smile. And he waited. And he waited. And he waited.

It was already 10 o'clock and not one customer had entered. All the usual people were still waiting outside Reb Yaakov's store.

"Go see why everyone is still standing on line over there!" he told his worker angrily.

The worker asked them, "Why are you standing here? The shop next door is already open and selling the same things."

"When we buy from this rabbi," they answered, "he always thanks us and gives us a special blessing. That's why we wait for him."

Hashem made sure that Rabbi Yaakov Yagen would not lose anything by learning Torah. If we do what is right, Hashem will always take care of us.

True Tefillah

Rav Shimshon Pincus was known for his warmth and his kindness. One evening, there was a soft knock at his door. A worried man stood on his doorstep.

"Come in, come in!" the Rav said. "Let's go to my study."

"My name is Refael," the man said. "My wife Rivkah and I have been married for five years and we do not have children." Tears streamed down his face. "Rav Pincus!" he cried. "We dream of a family of our own. But the doctors have given up on us. They say there is nothing they can do."

The Rav closed his eyes and thought. "Refael, I am going to ask you to do something strange. Come back to my house at 2 o'clock in the morning."

Refael was confused. "Why would the Rav want me to come back in the middle of the night?" But he was ready to do anything to have a child.

He arrived at 2 o'clock sharp. Rav Pincus brought him outside to his car.

Refael sat quietly in the car as they drove off to a place in the middle of nowhere. It was pitch black.

"I am leaving you now," Rav Pincus explained. "You will be all alone in the desert. Hashem is the only One here with you. Ask Him for children! Beg Him! Tell Him how sad you are! Tell Him how bad your wife feels! This is how you will have a child."

Rav Shimshon returned to his car. "I will be back in a half hour."

Refael *davened*. He begged Hashem for a child.

Half an hour later, he heard Rav Pincus's car.

"Refael," he said. "I see that you *davened*, but where are your tears? Hashem is your Father. Only He can help you! I'll be back in a half hour." Again, Refael was alone, only with Hashem.

He concentrated hard and began to cry. His body shook. Suddenly, he felt attached to Hashem! Hashem was part of him!

When Rav Pincus returned, Refael did not hear the car. He was crying and talking to Hashem. Rav Shimshon got out of his car and looked at him.

"This is true *tefillah*!" he whispered. "You were talking to Hashem and He loved every word." He took Refael's hand. "Come. You will see that your prayers will be answered."

Ten months later, Refael and Rivkah were the proud parents of a beautiful baby boy.

When we speak directly to Hashem, our tefillos become much more powerful.

Fiery Faith

A giant fire broke out in the town of Radin. It spread quickly.

"Help! Fire! Fire!" Women held their babies tightly. Men ran to fill buckets of water. "Quick! More water over here!" Everyone in Radin was busy fighting the fire.

At last, they put it out. But half the town had burned down.

The Chafetz Chaim lived in Radin. He saw that the fire had stopped right before his home! Every house before his had burned down!

The people whose houses had not burned down offered their homes to those who were now homeless. "Come live with us until you rebuild your own homes."

A year later, another fire broke out. Again the people shouted and ran through the streets bringing water. This time the fire spread on the other side of the town. It burned all the houses that weren't burned the last time, including the home of the Chafetz Chaim.

As the fire was being put out, everyone stood outside with their families.

Standing in the crowd was a young man named Chaim Sinai. He wanted to hear what the Chafetz Chaim would say about this.

He moved closer to the Rav. "Hashem, You are so kind!" the Chafetz Chaim whispered. "You decreed that every house in Radin should burn down. But You were kind. You didn't burn down the whole town at once. Rather, half of the town burned down last year, so that we could take in the other half as guests. This year, the other half of the town burned down and now we will be guests. Hashem, You are so merciful."

The young man was in awe. These were the Chafetz Chaim's words after his own home had gone up in flames. He saw the goodness in Hashem's ways even at such a terrible time.

We must be happy and thankful to Hashem whatever happens. We can always find good in everything – even when it all seems so bad.

The Mistaken Wash

Yosef Hoffman sold children's clothing to large stores all over America. In a few days, he would be visiting the office of a big chain of stores. He hoped they would order the clothing that he had bought from a factory in China. He needed to show them samples, and so he called the manager of that factory.

"Hello, Mr. Chang. By next Tuesday, I will need one sample of each item of clothing from my order. Please ship it to my home right away."

The phone connection was not clear, but Mr. Chang wrote down the order anyway. "Got it," he answered. "Two samples of each to your home."

On Tuesday, a large box arrived at Yosef's home.

"*Abba, Abba*!" his daughter called out. "There's a HUGE box for you from China!"

Yosef smiled. He opened the box and took out the clothes. To his shock, there was not *one,* but *two* samples of each item! The bill was twice as large as usual. Yosef tried not to be upset. "This must be what Hashem wants for me," he thought. He put on a smile and joined his family for dinner.

The phone rang. The customer he was meeting tomorrow was on the line.

"Listen, Mr. Hoffman," he said. "What I really want is to see how the clothes will look after they are washed. Can you have them washed for me by tomorrow?

"No problem!" Yosef replied. He put one of each sample in the laundry basket.

"Esther," he said to his wife. "I need a big favor. Will you please wash the clothing in the basket for me? I need it for my meeting tomorrow."

“Sure,” she replied. After dinner, she put it all in the washing machine.

Later that night, Yosef went to the laundry room to prepare the washed clothing for his meeting the next day. He took one look at the clothing and gasped. Everything had shrunk! They were supposed to have been hung up to dry, but his wife did not know that, and she put them in the dryer! Now they were completely ruined. He couldn’t show these to his customer.

Then Yosef remembered. He had a second set of samples sent to him by mistake. Immediately, it was all clear. Hashem doesn’t make mistakes. This was all a plan to save him from losing the business deal. Quickly, he washed the other set of samples and hung them up to dry. In the morning they were perfect! The store owner loved them and placed a large order.

Everything Hashem does is for the best! And sometimes, He even shows us how.

A Sweet Deed

Shimon had just moved into a new neighborhood. But he was unhappy. He was finding it hard to make friends with the boys who lived there.

He passed by the park and saw some kids playing baseball. "Hi, everyone," he called. No one paid much attention.

"What do you want?" Yitzy finally called back without even looking up.

"Could you let me into the game?" Shimon asked.

"Go to the outfield," Yitzy said, gruffly.

The game ended. The boys decided to go to the candy store. The owner, Mr. Diamond, was a friend of Shimon's father. Mr. Diamond was always very nice to Shimon. Besides, Shimon loved candy and he loved visiting the store.

Walking into the store made Shimon feel better. "Mr. Diamond is always so nice to me," he thought. "At least I have him as a friend."

But today, Mr. Diamond was in a bad mood. A child had knocked over his lollypop stand, cracking all of the Whirlypops. Another child had pulled the lever on the chocolate rum-ball machine, knocking them all over the floor. And Mr. Diamond's son had fallen at school and needed stitches. But when Shimon walked in, Mr. Diamond saw that Shimon felt sad. And so, he put on a big smile and walked over to him.

"Shimon!" he exclaimed, putting his arm around him. "It's so good to see you again! How have you been?"

Then he gave Shimon one of the broken Whirlypops for free.

"Come back anytime," he called with a smile as the boys left.

18

"Hey, Shimon," Yitzy said. "How do you know him?" Yitzy was clearly impressed.

"Wow, Shimon!" Avigdor said. "He sure likes *you* a lot!"

Shimon was shocked. They were finally speaking to him. Shyly, he explained to them how he knew Mr. Diamond.

"You're lucky!" Yitzy exclaimed. "Maybe you can get him to like us too. And maybe he'll give us *all* free Whirlypops!"

Shimon smiled. "I would love to."

"Hey, Shimon," Avigdor said. "How about a game of basketball? You can be on my team."

Shimon went to play, and he couldn't be happier.

Mr. Diamond did not know how much he had just helped a lonely boy. We often do not know what our kind words do for someone else. But we must know that a good word can change somebody's life forever.

Rock Solid Faith

Yitzchak was an orphan for many years. Now, at the age of 18, the yeshivah was his only home.

Yitzchak's friends grew older and began leaving the yeshivah. They were getting married and starting their own families. But not Yitzchak. He did not have any money to pay for a wedding.

"Yitzchak," his friends said, "Don't worry about a thing. We will raise all the money you need to get married."

His friends got very busy raising money. But no matter how much they tried, they could not collect very much.

"That's enough!" Yitzchak told his friends. "Don't try anymore. If Hashem wants me to get married, He will send me what I need."

Friday morning, he stood by the Kosel, tears streaming down his face. "Hashem, You are my *Abba*. I want to get married. Please, help me start a family."

He took out his small *Tehillim* and said every word from beginning to end. When he finished, he said, "Hashem, I will not turn to people anymore. I have only You." He began saying *Tehillim* again from the beginning.

He concentrated on the meaning of each word. Suddenly, there was a tap on his shoulder.

"You look so worried," the man said. "Is there any way I can help you?"

"No, thank you," Yitzchak answered. "I am speaking to Hashem. Only He can help me."

Yitzchak turned back around, placing his hands on the cold stones of the Kosel. For the third time, he spoke to Hashem. "I am an orphan. I want to get married. Help me!"

The man tapped Yitzchak on his shoulder again.

"Let me be your help. I will be Hashem's messenger," the man explained. "I had a big court case today. I promised Hashem that if I won, I would find an orphan and pay for his wedding. I won the case and Hashem brought us here together, so I can help you."

The prophet Yirmiyahu teaches us, "בָּרוּךְ הַגֶּבֶר אֲשֶׁר יִבְטַח בַּה׳ וְהָיָה ה׳ מִבְטַחוֹ!"*, the person who places his trust only in Hashem will be blessed. We must feel as if we are orphans, and that only Hashem will help us. And He will.*

Drive Your Route

Even as a young boy, Yair always wanted to be a bus driver. He imagined himself driving a bus in Israel, zooming around the corners and speeding through the tight streets. Lots of people would be happily waiting for his bus to arrive.

When Yair was old enough he got a job as a bus driver.

At his first stop, he opened the door and picked up his first three passengers. He was so excited. But, as he drove along, he realized that very few people lived along his route.

The next day, the same thing happened. Yair was so disappointed. This wasn't his dream. Then, a crowded bus pulled up next to him. "That is the kind of bus I want. That is the type of bus driver I dreamed of becoming."

Yair had an idea. "Tomorrow, I will drive where I want, where I know there are people who need a bus."

The next day, he picked up dozens of children, mothers, strollers, and men. At the end of the day, Yair placed a large pouch of money on his boss's desk. He was so proud of himself.

Yair arrived at work early the next morning, happy as could be. "Come into my office, Yair. Right now," his boss yelled.

Yair smiled. He was ready to be complimented for his fine work. He saw yesterday's pouch of money sitting on the boss's desk.

"Yair, how did you bring in so much money? No driver on your route ever did that."

Proudly, Yair explained. "There were hardly any people on my route, so

I went to other streets where there were lots of people. I picked them up and brought them where they wanted to go."

"YOU WHAT?!" his boss shouted. "This is terrible! Your job is to pick up the passengers on your route. Whoever was waiting on your route wasn't picked up."

This story is a mashal (parable). It never really happened. But it teaches us a lesson. Hashem gives each of us our own job, and that is what we must do. That is what will make us happy and make Hashem proud.

Paid in Full

Yehuda finished his breakfast. Then he began to write. "I raked the leaves two days ago. I can charge $2.00 for that. I gave Daniel a bath. That should be worth $1.75."

He scratched his head. "Hmm. What else did I do?" Looking around, he spotted the garbage can in the corner of the kitchen. "Taking out the garbage. For sure that's worth $1.00. Playing with Daniel last night while Mommy made dinner – $2.00. Making my bed today. At least $3.00."

Yehuda was a very good 12-year-old boy who just needed money for all the great things he wanted to buy.

"My report card. With lots of A's and just two B's. $5.00."

Yehuda left the note on the table for his mother and ran off to catch his school bus.

An hour after Yehuda left, his mother saw the note. She was holding baby Daniel. Slipping him into his highchair, she read it:

Dear Mommy,

Raked the leaves — $2.00
Gave Daniel a bath — $1.75
Took out the garbage — $1.00
Played with Daniel — $2.00
Made my bed — $3.00
Good report card — $5.00

For all the things I did for you, you owe me: $14.75

Yours truly,
Yehuda

$2.00
$1.75
the garbage - $1.00
bed - $3.00
with younger brother -
$2.00
Report Card - $5.00
for you
owe me $4.75
From Yonason
Orange
Juice

She was shocked. "I can't believe this. Yehuda is charging me for taking out the garbage and for giving his brother a bath. Where is his gratitude for everything I do for him each day?"

She had an idea. Flipping over Yehuda's note, she wrote:

Dear Yehuda,

Cleaning up after your breakfast — no charge
Buying your shoes — no charge
Three meals every day — no charge
Summer camp — no charge
Birthday party — no charge
Driving you to your friends' houses — no charge
Doing your laundry — no charge
For all the love I give you — you owe me nothing.

Love, Mommy

She folded the note and put it back on the kitchen table.

When Yehuda came home, he ran to the kitchen. "I bet there is $12.00 in here for me," he thought as he unfolded the note. "Maybe even more."

Then he read his mother's note, and felt ashamed.

Tears rolled down his cheeks. He turned over the note and wrote, "PAID, PAID, PAID." Then he ran to his mother and gave her a big hug.

Sometimes, a person says to Hashem, "I gave so much tzedakah, or I davened with kavanah – so please, give me everything I want! Hashem gives us much more than we deserve. If we think about how much we have we will realize He doesn't owe us anything.

The Gift of Giving

Aharon read the *pasuk* again. "Beautiful!" Rabbi Steinman said. "Now let's review it again."

He was learning his bar mitzvah *parashah* with one of the best teachers in his city. Aharon was an only child, and his parents wanted only the best for him.

Finally, his bar mitzvah day arrived. Aharon woke up extra early and got dressed in his new suit. His father was already wearing his tallis and waiting downstairs, anxious to go to shul.

When they arrived, Aharon saw another boy already there with his father. "Why is he here so early?" he wondered.

Suddenly the *gabbai* noticed Aharon and gasped out loud. "Oh no! How could this be? How could I have made such a mistake? I told that boy over there that *he* can *lein* this week's *parashah*. It's his bar mitzvah also. How did I forget about you?"

Aharon's face turned white.

"Aharon, of course, you will be *leining* this *parashah*. We knew about this for so long. I will tell the other boy that he cannot *lein*. I feel terrible," he said.

Aharon heard what the *gabbai* said. He thought about all the months he had studied for this. He also thought about how hard the other boy had practiced. Aharon could not remain silent.

He walked over to the *gabbai*, "Please let that boy *lein*. That is what I want."

The *gabbai* was amazed. Aharon walked to his seat. His father put his arm around him. He was so proud of him. Aharon thought, "All my preparation was worth it if I could make someone else happy!" And with that, Aharon opened up his siddur and began to *daven*.

A year passed. Aharon's mother became very sick. She was in the hospital and Aharon was with her. Early Shabbos morning, there was noise in the hallway. Aharon left his mother's bedside and approached a man standing in the hallway and asked what was going on.

"Rav Elyashiv is here in this hospital over Shabbos," the man explained. "We have a *minyan* for him, but we forgot to get someone who could read the Torah."

"I can *lein* this *parashah,*" Aharon said. "It is my bar mitzvah *parashah*."

"Are you sure? Do you know it well?"

"Yes, yes," Aharon replied.

"So then let's go. Follow me!"

Aharon told his mother where he was going. She insisted on coming to hear her son *lein* for the first time.

Aharon *leined* beautifully for the *gadol hador*. "Why are you here in the hospital?" Rav Elyashiv asked after he thanked him. Aharon pointed to his weak mother who was sitting outside the doorway, listening. Rav Elyashiv called her inside.

"What a special son you have," he told her. "May Hashem grant you a long and healthy life filled with *nachas*."

Aharon's mother heard this and began to cry. She told Rav Elyashiv that it had taken her many years to have a child. Aharon was born after Rav Elyashiv had blessed her over fifteen years ago. She then told the Rav the story of his bar mitzvah day.

Rav Elyashiv's berachah helped Aharon's mother get well. Hashem gave Aharon the zechus to lein for the gadol hador. All this because he let someone lein instead of him at his bar mitzvah. Hashem rewards us for every mitzvah we do.

Guaranteed

Shimon Schorr loved to give money to poor people. But he had recently lost most of his fortune.

"What will I do?" he thought sadly. "How will I be able to keep giving *tzedakah?"*

He had an idea. He went to visit his old friend, Elchonon.

"I just lost a lot of money," Shimon explained. "But I have a few investments that will make money in two years. Until then, I need your help to continue giving *tzedakah*. Would you be willing to lend me 2 million dollars for two years?"

"That's a lot of money," Shimon said. "But I know you so I will do it. Who will guarantee to pay me back in case you can't?"

Shimon shook his head. "I don't have anyone. I don't want people to know that I lost all my money."

Elchonon was shocked. "How can I lend you so much money that I may never get back?"

"I am doing this for Hashem," Shimon said. "I am doing it to help His poor people. Hashem will guarantee it."

Elchonon's face lit up. "You are right! We will make Hashem our Guarantor." He wrote a check and gave it to a very happy Shimon.

Two years passed. Shimon went to see Elchonon, who greeted him with a warm smile.

"Elchonon," Shimon said, "I am sorry but I need two more months. Then, I will pay back every penny."

"Fine!" Elchonon said. The two friends spoke for a while and Shimon went back home feeling relieved.

Elchonon took out his siddur and spoke directly to Hashem. "You are the Guarantor for Shimon's loan. He doesn't have the money, but really, I don't want the money. I need a husband for my daughter, Mindy. Please, send her a husband and I will consider Shimon's debt fully paid."

Three weeks later, Mindy became a *kallah.*

"Thank you, Hashem!" Elchonon smiled. "And last week I finished a deal that brought in as much money as I lent Shimon. His debt is now fully paid!"

Two months later, Shimon returned to Elchonon's home with a big smile. "I am here to repay the loan, just as I promised."

"The loan? Hashem has already paid me. You do not owe me anything." Elchonon explained how Hashem had already paid him back.

"But I want to pay you back," Shimon said. "This is not my money!"

"I explained to you already that Hashem paid me. Let's go to *beis din* and they will decide."

Two days later, Shimon and Elchonon stood before *beis din* and told their story.

Rabbi Zicherman, one of the rabbanim, stood up. "Elchonon claims he was fully paid back by Hashem. Shimon claims he still needs to pay. The *beis din* has decided to return the money to the Guarantor, to Hashem. It is now a *Shemittah* year. This money will go to the farmers in *Eretz Yisrael* who are keeping *Shemittah*."

We trust our parents to help us. Hashem is our loving Father. When we place our trust in Him, He does not let us down. Guaranteed.

The Berachah

Avraham's youngest daughter, Hadassah, was very ill. There was only one doctor who could heal people with her illness. But he lived in the United States and it was impossible to get an appointment with him.

Avraham was learning *gemara* when the phone rang. "Yes? Now? Where? For how long? Half an hour? But I live in Jerusalem. Tel Aviv is an hour away. Okay. I'm coming now."

Avraham rushed to the door. "What's going on?" his wife called.

"The doctor from America is in Tel Aviv. He leaves in half an hour. If he sees me, maybe he will agree to meet with Hadassah."

Avraham jumped into the first taxi he saw. "Please, I must get to Tel Aviv in half an hour."

The taxi driver looked at him. "Impossible."

"Please," Avraham begged. He held up 300 shekels for the driver to see.

"Okay. For 300 shekels, I will do it."

The driver drove very fast and took all kinds of shortcuts. Finally, the taxi stopped in front of the building where the doctor was staying. It had taken just 29 minutes.

Avraham gave the money to the driver and raced up the steps.

"I am so sorry. He left just a minute ago," the man there told him.

Avraham looked like he was about to faint. People brought a chair and a cup of water. Avraham held the cup and made the *berachah, Shehakol.* He concentrated on the meaning of the words, knowing and feeling that everything is from Hashem. Then he said, "Hashem, You are everywhere. You are here whenever I need You.

Forget about the doctors. I have You! You are all I need. Please save my daughter."

"Are you okay?" the man asked him, very concerned.

Avraham smiled and looked at the people crowding around. "I have never been this okay in my life," he answered.

A few weeks later, Avraham brought his daughter Hadassah to a doctor. "It's amazing," the doctor said while looking over her tests. "This never happens."

The doctor showed the papers to Avraham. "The medicine we gave your daughter has started to work. She will be completely healthy in just a few weeks."

Avraham looked over to Hadassah with a big smile. Then he looked up to Hashem, feeling grateful. "Abba," Hadassah asked, "how come I'm going to get better if the doctor said no one ever does?"

Avraham told her about his trip to Tel Aviv and his talk with Hashem.

"But Abba," she asked. "Why did you have to go to Tel Aviv? You could have made the same *berachah* here in Jerusalem – in our own kitchen."

"That is true," he replied. "But if not for everything that happened that day, I could never have made that *berachah* with such concentration."

Sometimes life can be very difficult. But it is this struggle to overcome our problems that raises us to new levels of emunah.

The Missing Shoes

Moshe Barom arrived at Kennedy Airport after spending two weeks in New York, where he had tried to collect money for his youngest daughter's wedding. Sadly, although he needed $25,000, he was not able to raise anything near that amount.

"Go to Australia," a Rav told him. "I will give you a *berachah*. You will raise all the money you need there."

R' Moshe walked toward the security station at the airport, getting ready to pass through.

"Shoes off, bags here!" a security guard called out. Each person put their shoes and bags on the conveyor belt that then passed through the x-ray machine. R' Moshe then passed through the x-ray machine himself. When he went to get his bag and shoes, his shoes were nowhere to be found! The guard looked everywhere. All they found was another pair of shoes two sizes too small.

"I'm very sorry, sir," the guard said. "Someone must have taken them by mistake. I can give you a gift card to buy shoes in Australia." But then R' Moshe would have to travel to Australia without shoes.

He looked down at his feet. "Okay. Thank you," he said, and walked onto the plane wearing only socks.

During the long flight, R' Moshe walked up and down the aisle. A tall African-American man was standing there. He kept looking at R' Moshe's feet.

"I was behind you at the airport," he said. "How did you stay so calm? I would have screamed at them. I wish I could be more like you. You even said thank you to the guard." Then he asked R' Moshe, "Why are you going to Australia?"

R’ Moshe explained. “I’m marrying off my eleventh child and have to raise money for the wedding.”

“What?!” the man shouted. “That’s not right! Such a nice man should not have to beg people for money. How much do you need?”

“I need $25,000.”

Right then, the man wrote a check for $25,000 and gave it to R’ Moshe.

R’ Moshe could not believe it. He could not stop thanking him.

When he arrived in Australia, he bought a pair of shoes and took the next flight home to *Eretz Yisrael*. On the night of his daughter’s wedding, R’ Moshe danced wearing a wide smile on his face – and his brand new shoes.

When we act the way R’ Moshe did, we do a great Kiddush Hashem, and Hashem will surely send us the extra help we need.

Standing Strong

Rabbi Lazar looked at his watch. His El Al flight from Tel Aviv to New York was already two hours late. A man approached him. "Will you join us for *Minchah*?"

"Of course, of course," he replied.

As soon as they began *Shemoneh Esrei,* a message blared over the loudspeakers.

Flight 204 is now boarding to New York. Flight 204 is now boarding.

The men finished *Minchah*, grabbed their bags, and rushed to the plane. Rabbi Lazar saw a young woman still *davening,* concentrating deeply.

Rabbi Lazar went to a flight attendant. "That young woman is still praying. Would it be possible to wait for her?"

"Five minutes," Eli the attendant, replied. "Five minutes and we close the gates."

Five minutes passed and the woman was still *davening*.

Everyone except the girl had boarded when suddenly the attendant announced, "All passengers please get off the plane immediately. There is smoke in the back of the plane. Our workers will fix it shortly."

They all left the plane and sat back down in the waiting area. Finally, there was a new announcement to board the plane again.

Rabbi Lazar asked the young woman, "I hope you don't mind my asking, but how were you able to keep *davening* when you knew that the plane would be leaving without you?"

She blushed. "My name is Rachel. I am not married yet. When I became thirty years old, I decided from that day on to concentrate on

every word of *Shemoneh Esrei* and pray to Hashem for a husband. Today it was very hard for me to do, but I did it."

During the flight, Rabbi Lazar spoke to Eli, the flight attendant who had closed the gates. "What had caused the smoke in the plane?"

"Nobody knows," he answered. "But everything is fine and we can fly."

Rabbi Lazar told him the young woman's story. "Hashem sent the smoke so that she could make the flight."

"Wow!" Eli said. He was very moved at how Hashem had helped her.

Rabbi Lazar's eyes twinkled. "Eli, I would be so grateful if you would come to one of the classes I will be giving in New York. You will learn what makes a person truly happy."

Slowly, Eli began to learn things he had never heard before. He learned with Rabbi Lazar for many months, eventually becoming a full *baal teshuvah.*

One year later, Rabbi Lazar was honored to say a *berachah* under the *chuppah* at the wedding of Eli and Rachel. Her *Shemoneh Esrei* prayers had finally been answered.

Tefillah is a very powerful tool. It is very hard to daven when you are thinking of other things. But if you keep concentrating, your prayers become very powerful.

A Job and a Gem

Sarah wanted to be a teacher. But in Jerusalem, where she lived, there were very few teaching jobs available. Instead, every day, Sarah would visit people and do *chesed*.

"Hello, Mrs. Schmidt!" Sarah greeted the old woman that she visited every morning. "How are you? Here is your newspaper and coffee."

"Sarah, you are such a wonderful girl," Mrs. Schmidt smiled. "I know you want to teach. You should advertise in the paper for a teaching job. Maybe a principal will call you."

"That is a very good idea. I'll do it!"

Two days later, Sarah's phone rang. It was Rebbetzin Weinberg, the principal of the Bais Yaakov.

"Hello. Is this Sarah? I saw your ad in the newspaper today. I am looking for a teacher. Could you please meet with me?"

"Of course," Sarah said. They made up to meet the following week.

A few days later, Sarah saw her friend Esther in the grocery store.

"Sarah. It's so good to see you. I came here to pay part of the money we owe. We don't have enough money to shop here anymore. I wish I could find a teaching job to make some money."

"I know about a job," Sarah thought to herself, "but, I want it! The rebbetzin called me! I placed the ad. But Esther needs money for her family. I am still single. She is married with two children. She needs it more than I do."

Sarah smiled. "Today, I spoke to Rebbetzin Weinberg. She has a teaching job open. Why don't you call her?"

The next week, both Sarah and Esther went to meet the rebbetzin. A few days later, Rebbetzin Weinberg called Sarah and offered her the teaching job.

"What about my friend, Esther?" she asked.

"Esther also made a very good impression, but there is only one job available. Since you called me first, I'm offering the job to you."

"Esther needs this job much more than I do," Sarah said softly. "Please give it to her."

The rebbetzin was very surprised, but agreed to hire Esther instead.

One week later, Sarah's mother got a phone call from a friend about a *shidduch* for her daughter. "Listen, I have the best boy for Sarah and his mother asked me to speak to you directly," the woman said.

"Who is he?" Sarah's mother asked.

"Yechiel Weinberg, the son of the famous Rebbetzin Weinberg. She said she was so impressed that your daughter gave up a job offer for her friend. She said that is the kind of girl she wants for her son."

Sarah and Yechiel soon got married. And not long after, the rebbetzin found a job for Sarah in her school.

When we give up something we want so that we can help another person, Hashem always rewards us.